2021-2022

30 DAY WRITING NOTEBOOK

_____
_____
_____

from the creator of the bestselling Calendar For Writers Series

INDEPENDENTLY PUBLISHED

ANNUAL CALENDARS FOR 2021, 2022, & 2023 INCLUDED!

© Kimberly Coleman 2020

This is a uniquely designed and original calendar and writing notebook created, designed, and published by Irish Author Kimberly Coleman.
All rights strictly reserved.

ISBN: 9780578832203

Photo Credits
Front Cover © HunterXt www.fotosearch.ie
Title Page © ilasla www.fotosearch.ie
2021,2022,2023 Calendars © DmitryGuzhanin www.fotosearch.ie

---

*Cover and Interior Design by Kimberly Coleman,
creator of the Bestselling Calendar For Writers Series*

I've published my Calendar For Writers since late 2016 and through the years the format has, in general, remained the same but the contents evolve based on feedback from writers who find these beneficial to their creativity. Adding my new **30-Day Writing Notebook** is meant to expand options for writers wanting to explore how they can manage their writing time without interfering with the creativity of it. These are workbooks you will either love or hate. If you are a 'new' writer you may find yourself getting organized and starting to write more and better, sooner; if you are a more experienced writer, you might find the notebooks constrictive or remedial when they are simply meant to 'be there' for you, to give you a single place to stash your thoughts and notes and snips and articles… There is a lot to be said in our tech age for presence and simple functionality. These oversized notebooks harken back to the past when teens wanted a 'slam book' to scribble in or a reliable and sturdy (and fairly stain-resistant) stack of bound pages to carry with them. Whatever you seek for your writing life I hope you find it….often it comes down to the type of paper and style of ink pen (and ink color, etc.!) for myself. That calms my ADD for a bit and I can get on with my writing.
Thanks for reading :>

INDEPENDENTLY PUBLISHED

Take 30 days and write your novel!
Get your first draft on paper in 30 days with this Notebook...

This is a basic Notebook designed especially for those who want to write their novels in 30-Day time periods. You can set your own pace: your writing days do not have to be consecutive, but you should aim to complete one day's work within 24 hours. Think of it as 'sectional' or 'segmented' writing: there is a beginning, middle and end to your daily output. For many writers, this can work to prevent 'writer's block', wherein you have an idea, but it doesn't necessarily 'fit' where you are at the moment in your draft, but you go ahead and write that segment; moving it later, in your second or third draft .. The point is to get it all down for editing later.

Divided into Week 1 through Week 4, each section contains 7 days with 8 pages (37 narrow lines to a page) to write on for each day. The 29th and 30th days follow Week 4. Each page is designed with a 1-inch margin on the left, a Word Count box at the bottom, and extra white space for additional notes and/or color/sticky note highlights. A Planning Page is placed at the start of each week. Five additional pages for Notes are appended at the end.

Tips for *success*...
1) Create a writing sanctuary, a space all your own where you can return each day to write.

2) Try to schedule your writing time to minimize interruptions.

3) Keep dictionary/thesaurus, the books of authors who inspire you, your totems, etc., within reach while you write.

4) Check Twitter, Facebook, Instagram, etc., before beginning to write each day (and as soon as you finish, if you find that rewarding).

5) If you miss a day writing, simply return to it when you can: the 30 Days do not have to be consecutive. It is more important in the long run to continue writing, to tell your story, get it down on paper and in a concise, easily editable format. Once you finish this Notebook, go to your computer and begin typing from it: you will find yourself immediately back in your story and will readily see just where you need to start your editing.

WEEK 1

DAY 1

WORD COUNT:

DAY 1

WORD COUNT:

DAY 1

WORD COUNT:

DAY 1

WORD COUNT:

DAY 1

WORD COUNT:

DAY 1

WORD COUNT:

DAY 1

WORD COUNT:

DAY 1

WORD COUNT:

DAY 2

WORD COUNT:

DAY 2

WORD COUNT:

DAY 2

WORD COUNT:

DAY 2

WORD COUNT:

DAY 2

WORD COUNT:

DAY 2

WORD COUNT:

DAY 2

WORD COUNT:

DAY 2

WORD COUNT:

DAY 3

WORD COUNT:

DAY 3

WORD COUNT:

DAY 3

WORD COUNT:

DAY 3

WORD COUNT:

DAY 3

WORD COUNT:

DAY 3

WORD COUNT:

DAY 3

WORD COUNT:

DAY 3

WORD COUNT:

DAY 4

WORD COUNT:

DAY 4

WORD COUNT:

DAY 4

WORD COUNT:

DAY 4

WORD COUNT:

DAY 4

WORD COUNT:

DAY 4

WORD COUNT:

DAY 4

WORD COUNT:

DAY 4

WORD COUNT:

DAY 5

WORD COUNT:

DAY 5

WORD COUNT:

DAY 5

WORD COUNT:

DAY 5

WORD COUNT:

DAY 5

WORD COUNT:

DAY 5

WORD COUNT:

DAY 5

WORD COUNT:

DAY 5

WORD COUNT:

DAY 6

WORD COUNT:

DAY 6

WORD COUNT:

… DAY 6

WORD COUNT:

DAY 6

WORD COUNT:

DAY 6

WORD COUNT:

DAY 6

WORD COUNT:

DAY 6

WORD COUNT:

DAY 6

WORD COUNT:

DAY 7

WORD COUNT:

DAY 7

WORD COUNT:

DAY 7

WORD COUNT:

DAY 7

WORD COUNT:

DAY 7

WORD COUNT:

DAY 7

WORD COUNT:

DAY 7

WORD COUNT:

DAY 7

WORD COUNT:

WEEK 2

DAY 8

WORD COUNT:

DAY 8

WORD COUNT:

DAY 8

WORD COUNT:

DAY 8

WORD COUNT:

DAY 8

WORD COUNT:

DAY 8

WORD COUNT:

DAY 8

WORD COUNT:

DAY 8

WORD COUNT:

DAY 9

WORD COUNT:

DAY 9

WORD COUNT:

DAY 9

WORD COUNT:

DAY 9

WORD COUNT:

DAY 9

WORD COUNT:

DAY 9

WORD COUNT:

DAY 9

WORD COUNT:

DAY 9

WORD COUNT:

DAY 10

WORD COUNT:

DAY 10

WORD COUNT:

DAY 10

WORD COUNT:

DAY 10

WORD COUNT:

DAY 10

WORD COUNT:

DAY 10

WORD COUNT:

DAY 10

WORD COUNT:

DAY 10

WORD COUNT:

DAY 11

WORD COUNT:

DAY 11

WORD COUNT:

DAY 11

WORD COUNT:

DAY 11

WORD COUNT:

DAY 11

WORD COUNT:

DAY 11

WORD COUNT:

DAY 11

WORD COUNT:

DAY 11

WORD COUNT:

DAY 12

WORD COUNT:

DAY 12

WORD COUNT:

DAY 12

WORD COUNT:

DAY 12

WORD COUNT:

DAY 12

WORD COUNT:

DAY 12

WORD COUNT:

DAY 12

WORD COUNT:

DAY 12

WORD COUNT:

DAY 13

WORD COUNT:

DAY 13

WORD COUNT:

DAY 13

WORD COUNT:

DAY 13

WORD COUNT:

DAY 13

WORD COUNT:

DAY 13

WORD COUNT:

DAY 13

WORD COUNT:

DAY 13

WORD COUNT:

DAY 14

WORD COUNT:

DAY 14

WORD COUNT:

DAY 14

WORD COUNT:

DAY 14

WORD COUNT:

DAY 14

WORD COUNT:

DAY 14

WORD COUNT:

DAY 14

WORD COUNT:

DAY 14

WORD COUNT:

WEEK 3

DAY 15

WORD COUNT:

DAY 15

WORD COUNT:

DAY 15

WORD COUNT:

DAY 15

WORD COUNT:

DAY 15

WORD COUNT:

DAY 15

WORD COUNT:

DAY 15

WORD COUNT:

DAY 15

WORD COUNT:

DAY 16

WORD COUNT:

DAY 16

WORD COUNT:

DAY 16

WORD COUNT:

DAY 16

WORD COUNT:

DAY 16

WORD COUNT:

DAY 16

WORD COUNT:

DAY 16

WORD COUNT:

DAY 16

WORD COUNT:

DAY 17

WORD COUNT:

DAY 17

WORD COUNT:

DAY 17

WORD COUNT:

DAY 17

WORD COUNT:

DAY 17

WORD COUNT:

DAY 17

WORD COUNT:

DAY 17

WORD COUNT:

DAY 17

WORD COUNT:

DAY 18

WORD COUNT:

DAY 18

WORD COUNT:

DAY 18

WORD COUNT:

DAY 18

WORD COUNT:

DAY 18

WORD COUNT:

DAY 18

WORD COUNT:

DAY 18

WORD COUNT:

DAY 18

WORD COUNT:

DAY 19

WORD COUNT:

DAY 19

WORD COUNT:

DAY 19

WORD COUNT:

DAY 19

WORD COUNT:

DAY 19

WORD COUNT:

DAY 19

WORD COUNT:

DAY 19

WORD COUNT:

DAY 19

WORD COUNT:

DAY 20

WORD COUNT:

DAY 20

WORD COUNT:

DAY 20

WORD COUNT:

DAY 20

WORD COUNT:

DAY 20

WORD COUNT:

DAY 20

WORD COUNT:

DAY 20

WORD COUNT:

DAY 20

WORD COUNT:

DAY 21

WORD COUNT:

DAY 21

WORD COUNT:

DAY 21

WORD COUNT:

DAY 21

WORD COUNT:

DAY 21

WORD COUNT:

DAY 21

WORD COUNT:

DAY 21

WORD COUNT:

DAY 21

WORD COUNT:

WEEK 4

DAY 22

WORD COUNT:

DAY 22

WORD COUNT:

DAY 22

WORD COUNT:

DAY 22

WORD COUNT:

DAY 22

WORD COUNT:

DAY 22

WORD COUNT:

DAY 22

WORD COUNT:

DAY 22

WORD COUNT:

DAY 23

WORD COUNT:

DAY 23

WORD COUNT:

DAY 23

WORD COUNT:

DAY 23

WORD COUNT:

DAY 23

WORD COUNT:

DAY 23

WORD COUNT:

DAY 23

WORD COUNT:

DAY 23

WORD COUNT:

DAY 24

WORD COUNT:

DAY 24

WORD COUNT:

DAY 24

WORD COUNT:

DAY 24

WORD COUNT:

DAY 24

WORD COUNT:

DAY 24

WORD COUNT:

DAY 24

WORD COUNT:

DAY 24

WORD COUNT:

DAY 25

WORD COUNT:

DAY 25

WORD COUNT:

DAY 25

WORD COUNT:

DAY 25

WORD COUNT:

DAY 25

WORD COUNT:

DAY 25

WORD COUNT:

DAY 25

WORD COUNT:

DAY 25

WORD COUNT:

DAY 26

WORD COUNT:

DAY 26

WORD COUNT:

DAY 26

WORD COUNT:

DAY 26

WORD COUNT:

DAY 26

WORD COUNT:

DAY 26

WORD COUNT:

DAY 26

WORD COUNT:

DAY 26

WORD COUNT:

DAY 27

WORD COUNT:

DAY 27

WORD COUNT:

DAY 27

WORD COUNT:

DAY 27

WORD COUNT:

DAY 27

WORD COUNT:

DAY 27

WORD COUNT:

DAY 27

WORD COUNT:

DAY 27

WORD COUNT:

DAY 28

WORD COUNT:

DAY 28

WORD COUNT:

DAY 28

WORD COUNT:

DAY 28

WORD COUNT:

DAY 28

WORD COUNT:

DAY 28

WORD COUNT:

DAY 28

WORD COUNT:

DAY 28

WORD COUNT:

TWO MORE DAYS...

DAY 29

WORD COUNT:

DAY 29

WORD COUNT:

DAY 29

WORD COUNT:

DAY 29

WORD COUNT:

DAY 29

WORD COUNT:

DAY 29

WORD COUNT:

DAY 29

WORD COUNT:

DAY 29

WORD COUNT:

DAY 30

WORD COUNT:

DAY 30

WORD COUNT:

DAY 30

WORD COUNT:

DAY 30

WORD COUNT:

DAY 30

WORD COUNT:

DAY 30

WORD COUNT:

DAY 30

WORD COUNT:

DAY 30

WORD COUNT:

NOTES

2021

January
Su	Mo	Tu	We	Th	Fr	Sa
					1	2
3	4	5	6	7	8	9
10	11	12	13	14	15	16
17	18	19	20	21	22	23
24	25	26	27	28	29	30
31						

February
Su	Mo	Tu	We	Th	Fr	Sa
	1	2	3	4	5	6
7	8	9	10	11	12	13
14	15	16	17	18	19	20
21	22	23	24	25	26	27
28						

March
Su	Mo	Tu	We	Th	Fr	Sa
	1	2	3	4	5	6
7	8	9	10	11	12	13
14	15	16	17	18	19	20
21	22	23	24	25	26	27
28	29	30	31			

April
Su	Mo	Tu	We	Th	Fr	Sa
				1	2	3
4	5	6	7	8	9	10
11	12	13	14	15	16	17
18	19	20	21	22	23	24
25	26	27	28	29	30	

May
Su	Mo	Tu	We	Th	Fr	Sa
						1
2	3	4	5	6	7	8
9	10	11	12	13	14	15
16	17	18	19	20	21	22
23	24	25	26	27	28	29
30	31					

June
Su	Mo	Tu	We	Th	Fr	Sa
		1	2	3	4	5
6	7	8	9	10	11	12
13	14	15	16	17	18	19
20	21	22	23	24	25	26
27	28	29	30			

July
Su	Mo	Tu	We	Th	Fr	Sa
				1	2	3
4	5	6	7	8	9	10
11	12	13	14	15	16	17
18	19	20	21	22	23	24
25	26	27	28	29	30	31

August
Su	Mo	Tu	We	Th	Fr	Sa
1	2	3	4	5	6	7
8	9	10	11	12	13	14
15	16	17	18	19	20	21
22	23	24	25	26	27	28
29	30	31				

September
Su	Mo	Tu	We	Th	Fr	Sa
			1	2	3	4
5	6	7	8	9	10	11
12	13	14	15	16	17	18
19	20	21	22	23	24	25
26	27	28	29	30		

October
Su	Mo	Tu	We	Th	Fr	Sa
					1	2
3	4	5	6	7	8	9
10	11	12	13	14	15	16
17	18	19	20	21	22	23
24	25	26	27	28	29	30
31						

November
Su	Mo	Tu	We	Th	Fr	Sa
	1	2	3	4	5	6
7	8	9	10	11	12	13
14	15	16	17	18	19	20
21	22	23	24	25	26	27
28	29	30				

December
Su	Mo	Tu	We	Th	Fr	Sa
			1	2	3	4
5	6	7	8	9	10	11
12	13	14	15	16	17	18
19	20	21	22	23	24	25
26	27	28	29	30	31	

2022

January
Su	Mo	Tu	We	Th	Fr	Sa
						1
2	3	4	5	6	7	8
9	10	11	12	13	14	15
16	17	18	19	20	21	22
23	24	25	26	27	28	29
30	31					

February
Su	Mo	Tu	We	Th	Fr	Sa
		1	2	3	4	5
6	7	8	9	10	11	12
13	14	15	16	17	18	19
20	21	22	23	24	25	26
27	28					

March
Su	Mo	Tu	We	Th	Fr	Sa
		1	2	3	4	5
6	7	8	9	10	11	12
13	14	15	16	17	18	19
20	21	22	23	24	25	26
27	28	29	30	31		

April
Su	Mo	Tu	We	Th	Fr	Sa
					1	2
3	4	5	6	7	8	9
10	11	12	13	14	15	16
17	18	19	20	21	22	23
24	25	26	27	28	29	30

May
Su	Mo	Tu	We	Th	Fr	Sa
1	2	3	4	5	6	7
8	9	10	11	12	13	14
15	16	17	18	19	20	21
22	23	24	25	26	27	28
29	30	31				

June
Su	Mo	Tu	We	Th	Fr	Sa
			1	2	3	4
5	6	7	8	9	10	11
12	13	14	15	16	17	18
19	20	21	22	23	24	25
26	27	28	29	30		

July
Su	Mo	Tu	We	Th	Fr	Sa
					1	2
3	4	5	6	7	8	9
10	11	12	13	14	15	16
17	18	19	20	21	22	23
24	25	26	27	28	29	30
31						

August
Su	Mo	Tu	We	Th	Fr	Sa
	1	2	3	4	5	6
7	8	9	10	11	12	13
14	15	16	17	18	19	20
21	22	23	24	25	26	27
28	29	30	31			

September
Su	Mo	Tu	We	Th	Fr	Sa
				1	2	3
4	5	6	7	8	9	10
11	12	13	14	15	16	17
18	19	20	21	22	23	24
25	26	27	28	29	30	

October
Su	Mo	Tu	We	Th	Fr	Sa
						1
2	3	4	5	6	7	8
9	10	11	12	13	14	15
16	17	18	19	20	21	22
23	24	25	26	27	28	29
30	31					

November
Su	Mo	Tu	We	Th	Fr	Sa
		1	2	3	4	5
6	7	8	9	10	11	12
13	14	15	16	17	18	19
20	21	22	23	24	25	26
27	28	29	30			

December
Su	Mo	Tu	We	Th	Fr	Sa
				1	2	3
4	5	6	7	8	9	10
11	12	13	14	15	16	17
18	19	20	21	22	23	24
25	26	27	28	29	30	31

2023

January
Su	Mo	Tu	We	Th	Fr	Sa
1	2	3	4	5	6	7
8	9	10	11	12	13	14
15	16	17	18	19	20	21
22	23	24	25	26	27	28
29	30	31				

February
Su	Mo	Tu	We	Th	Fr	Sa
			1	2	3	4
5	6	7	8	9	10	11
12	13	14	15	16	17	18
19	20	21	22	23	24	25
26	27	28				

March
Su	Mo	Tu	We	Th	Fr	Sa
			1	2	3	4
5	6	7	8	9	10	11
12	13	14	15	16	17	18
19	20	21	22	23	24	25
26	27	28	29	30	31	

April
Su	Mo	Tu	We	Th	Fr	Sa
						1
2	3	4	5	6	7	8
9	10	11	12	13	14	15
16	17	18	19	20	21	22
23	24	25	26	27	28	29
30						

May
Su	Mo	Tu	We	Th	Fr	Sa
	1	2	3	4	5	6
7	8	9	10	11	12	13
14	15	16	17	18	19	20
21	22	23	24	25	26	27
28	29	30	31			

June
Su	Mo	Tu	We	Th	Fr	Sa
				1	2	3
4	5	6	7	8	9	10
11	12	13	14	15	16	17
18	19	20	21	22	23	24
25	26	27	28	29	30	

July
Su	Mo	Tu	We	Th	Fr	Sa
						1
2	3	4	5	6	7	8
9	10	11	12	13	14	15
16	17	18	19	20	21	22
23	24	25	26	27	28	29
30	31					

August
Su	Mo	Tu	We	Th	Fr	Sa
		1	2	3	4	5
6	7	8	9	10	11	12
13	14	15	16	17	18	19
20	21	22	23	24	25	26
27	28	29	30	31		

September
Su	Mo	Tu	We	Th	Fr	Sa
					1	2
3	4	5	6	7	8	9
10	11	12	13	14	15	16
17	18	19	20	21	22	23
24	25	26	27	28	29	30

October
Su	Mo	Tu	We	Th	Fr	Sa
1	2	3	4	5	6	7
8	9	10	11	12	13	14
15	16	17	18	19	20	21
22	23	24	25	26	27	28
29	30	31				

November
Su	Mo	Tu	We	Th	Fr	Sa
			1	2	3	4
5	6	7	8	9	10	11
12	13	14	15	16	17	18
19	20	21	22	23	24	25
26	27	28	29	30		

December
Su	Mo	Tu	We	Th	Fr	Sa
					1	2
3	4	5	6	7	8	9
10	11	12	13	14	15	16
17	18	19	20	21	22	23
24	25	26	27	28	29	30
31						

Also available

1,000 Quotes For Writers by Kimberly Coleman

2021 Calendar For Writers

2021 Calendar For Writers Writing Notebook Expanded Edition

30-Day Writing Notebook

Available worldwide in eBook and Print formats.

www.ingramcontent.com/pod-product-compliance
Lightning Source LLC
Chambersburg PA
CBHW081151290426
44108CB00018B/2513